Classic Tales

Level 3

CW00891107

Little Red Riding Hood

Retold by Sue Arengo

Illustrated by Michelle Lamoreaux

Contents

OXFORD
UNIVERSITY PRESS

This is the story of a little girl, her grandma, and a big bad wolf.

The little girl lived in a little white house. The house was in a village and the village was near a forest.

She was a good little girl. Her mother and father loved her very much. Her grandma loved her very much too.

The little girl's grandma lived in a very old house in the middle of the forest. The little girl often went to her grandma's house.

One Christmas, Grandma gave the little girl a beautiful red cloak with a hood.

'Oh, thank you!' said the little girl.

She wore the cloak all day on Christmas Day, and the next day too. She wore it all the time, so people gave her a new name. They called her 'Little Red Riding Hood'.

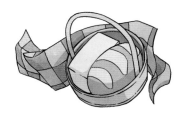

One day her mother said, 'Little Red Riding Hood, your grandma is ill. Go to her house and take her this basket of bread and butter. Walk quickly to her house. Don't stop and play. And don't leave the road. Do you understand?'

'Yes, Mother,' said Little Red Riding Hood.

Little Red Riding Hood took the basket and ran into the forest.

She walked very quickly. She did not stop and play. But soon after, she saw …

… a wolf!

'Hello,' said the wolf. 'How are you today?'

'I'm very well, thank you,' she answered. 'But my grandma is ill. I'm taking this basket of bread and butter to her.'

'Are you?' said the wolf. 'That's interesting!'

The wolf was very hungry. He looked at Little Red Riding Hood with his big hungry eyes.

'Where does your grandma live?' he asked.

'She lives in a little old house in the middle of the forest,' said Little Red Riding Hood.

'Is it far?'

'No. It's very near here.'

'Mmm,' thought the wolf. 'Perhaps I can eat this little girl *and* her grandma.'

'Look over there!' said the wolf. 'Can you see those nice flowers? Does your grandma like flowers? You can go and get some for her.'

'Oh no, I can't,' said Little Red Riding Hood. 'I can't leave the road.'

'But you can come back to the road later,' said the wolf.

'Yes … that's true,' said Little Red Riding Hood slowly. 'I can. Oh, all right!'

So she walked through the trees to the flowers.

Now the bad wolf ran quickly to
Grandma's house.

He went to the door and knocked.

'Who is it?' called Little Red Riding Hood's
grandma.

'It's me, Grandma!' the wolf answered.
'It's Little Red Riding Hood!'

'Open the door and come in, dear.'

'Where are you, Grandma?' called the wolf.

'I'm upstairs in bed, dear. I am ill today and I can't get up.'

'I've got some nice bread and butter for you,' called the wolf.

He went up the stairs and ran into Grandma's bedroom. Then he jumped onto the bed and opened his big mouth and ate her!

The wolf put on one of Grandma's nightdresses, and got into her bed and waited. He waited for Little Red Riding Hood.

Little Red Riding Hood got lots of beautiful flowers in the forest.

Then suddenly she remembered her grandma.

'Oh dear!' she said. 'I'm going to be late!'

She ran back to the road, and soon she came to her grandma's house. She stopped when she saw the open door.

'That's strange,' thought Little Red Riding Hood. 'Why is Grandma's door open?' And she went in.

The wolf heard Little Red Riding Hood.

'Who is it?' he called.

'It's me, Grandma! It's Little Red Riding Hood.'

'I'm upstairs in bed, dear,' called the wolf. 'I am ill today and I can't get up.'

So Little Red Riding Hood went up the stairs.

'Grandma's voice is very strange today!' she thought. 'It's because she is ill.'

Little Red Riding Hood went into the bedroom.

'Hello, Grandma,' she said. 'I am sorry you are ill today. Look! I've got some nice bread and butter for you. And some beautiful flowers!'

'Thank you, dear,' said the wolf. 'Put them on the table and come here.'

So Little Red Riding Hood put down her basket and went to the bed.

'Oh, Grandma,' she said, 'you look very strange today!'

And suddenly she was afraid.

'Oh, Grandma,' said Little Red Riding Hood, 'you've got very big eyes today!'

'That's because I want to see you, my dear,' said the wolf.

'Oh, Grandma,' said Little Red Riding Hood, 'you've got very big ears today!'

'That's because I want to hear you, my dear,' said the wolf.

'Oh, Grandma, you've got a very big nose today!'

'That's because I want to smell those beautiful flowers, my dear.'

'Oh, Grandma!' said Little Red Riding Hood, 'you've got a very big mouth today, and a lot of very big teeth!'

'Yes, my dear,' said the wolf. 'And that's because I want to eat you!'

And the wolf jumped out of the bed and ate Little Red Riding Hood.

Now the wolf was big and fat and he wanted to go to sleep. He took off Grandma's nightdress and put it on the floor.

Then he got back into bed and went to sleep. Soon he began to snore loudly.

'Zhhhh,' he snored. 'Zhhhhh!'

Soon after, Little Red Riding Hood's father came to the house. He saw the open door.

'That's strange,' he thought. 'Why is the door open? And what's that noise?'

'Zhhhhhh,' snored the wolf. 'Zhhhhhhh!'

'Grandma's voice is very strange today,' thought Little Red Riding Hood's father.

He went upstairs to Grandma's bedroom.
He looked at the bed and saw the wolf.

'It's you!' he said. He knew about the wolf.
All the men in the village wanted to find it
and kill it.

'What are you doing in Grandma's bed? Well,
you can't run away now.'

And he took his knife and killed the wolf.

Then he thought, 'Perhaps Grandma is alive!'

So Little Red Riding Hood's father took his knife and cut open the wolf. And Little Red Riding Hood jumped out.

'Oh, Father! Quick! Help Grandma. She's in there, in the dark!'

Then Grandma jumped out.

'Oh! Oh! Where's that bad wolf?' she said.

'Everything's all right now,' said Little Red Riding Hood's father. 'The wolf is dead.'

So Grandma had a cup of tea and some nice bread and butter.

Then Little Red Riding Hood and her father went home to their little white house. Little Red Riding Hood ran to her mother and told her everything.

'But it's all right now!' she said.

'Yes,' said her mother. 'But Little Red Riding Hood, do not talk to wolves again. And do not leave the road when you go through the forest. Do you understand?'

'Yes, Mother.'

After that, Little Red Riding Hood always stayed on the road. And she never saw a wolf again.

1 Who is speaking? Write the name for 1–4.
For number 5, what does Grandma say? Write one sentence.

1 'Little Red Riding Hood, your grandma is ill.'   _Mother_
2 'Perhaps I can eat this little girl *and* her grandma.'   _____
3 'Grandma, you've got very big eyes today!'   _____
4 'What are you doing in Grandma's bed?'   _____
5 _____   _Grandma_

2 Match, then complete the sentences with the past tense.

stay   run   see   tell   go   say

told   ran   stayed   said   went   saw

Little Red Riding Hood and her father ___*went*___ home to
their little white house. Little Red Riding Hood _____
to her mother and _____ her everything.

'But it's all right now!' she
_____.

After that, Little Red Riding
Hood always _____
on the road. And she never
_____ a wolf again.

3 Make sentences about the story.
Then write them in the correct order.

Little Red Riding Hood ran to her mother and ...	ate Little Red Riding Hood.
The wolf jumped out of the bed and ...	ran into the forest.
Little Red Riding Hood's father took his knife and ...	told her everything.
Little Red Riding Hood took the basket and ...	killed the wolf.

1 *Little Red Riding Hood took the basket and ran into the forest.*

2 _____

3 _____

4 _____

4 Write the words.

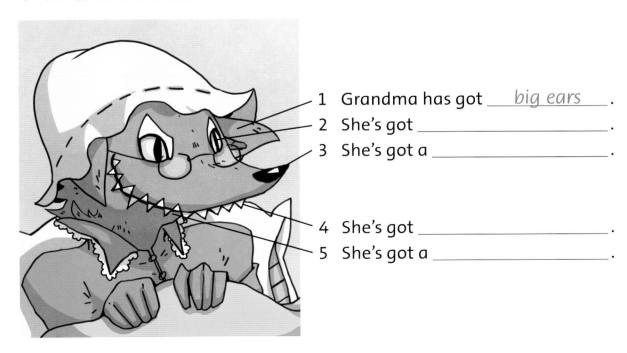

1 Grandma has got ___big ears___ .

2 She's got _____ .

3 She's got a _____ .

4 She's got _____ .

5 She's got a _____ .

Glossary

afraid *She is afraid.*

alive not dead

basket

bread

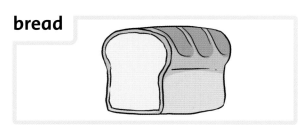

butter

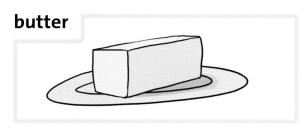

cloak

cup

cut open

dark not light; at night the sky is dark

dead not alive; when someone / something has died

floor

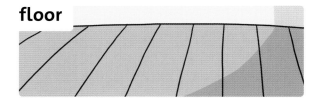

forest a place with many trees

grandma the mother of your mother or father

hood

ill not well

kill to make someone / something die

knife

loudly making a lot of noise

middle *The box is in the middle.*

nightdress

noise a loud sound; something you hear

road

run away to leave quickly; to escape

smell

snore to make a loud noise when you are sleeping

stairs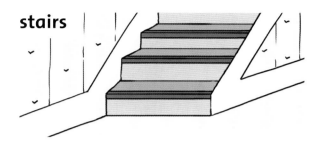

strange unusual and different

tea

teeth

village a very small town in the country

voice the sound from your mouth when you speak or sing

wolf

wore past tense of **wear**: to have clothes on your body

Classic Tales

Classic stories retold for learners of English – bringing the magic of traditional storytelling to the language classroom

Level 1: 100 headwords
- The Enormous Turnip
- The Little Red Hen
- Lownu Mends the Sky
- The Magic Cooking Pot
- Mansour and the Donkey
- Peach Boy
- The Princess and the Pea
- Rumpelstiltskin
- The Shoemaker and the Elves
- Three Billy-Goats

Level 2: 150 headwords
- Amrita and the Trees
- Big Baby Finn
- The Fisherman and his Wife
- The Gingerbread Man
- Jack and the Beanstalk
- Thumbelina
- The Town Mouse and the Country Mouse
- The Ugly Duckling

Level 3: 200 headwords
- Aladdin
- Goldilocks and the Three Bears
- The Heron and the Hummingbird
- The Little Mermaid
- Little Red Riding Hood
- Rapunzel

Level 4: 300 headwords
- Cinderella
- The Goose Girl
- Sleeping Beauty
- The Twelve Dancing Princesses

Level 5: 400 headwords
- Beauty and the Beast
- The Magic Brocade
- Pinocchio
- Snow White and the Seven Dwarfs

All *Classic Tales* have an accompanying
- **e-Book with Audio Pack** containing the book and the e-book with audio, for use on a computer or CD player. Teachers can also project the e-book onto an interactive whiteboard to use it like a Big Book.
- **Activity Book and Play** providing extra language practice and the story adapted as a play for performance in class or on stage.

For more details, visit
www.oup.com/elt/teacher/classictales

OXFORD
UNIVERSITY PRESS

Great Clarendon Street, Oxford OX2 6DP

Oxford University Press is a department of the University of Oxford. It furthers the University's objective of excellence in research, scholarship, and education by publishing worldwide in

Oxford New York

Auckland Cape Town Dar es Salaam Hong Kong Karachi Kuala Lumpur Madrid Melbourne Mexico City Nairobi New Delhi Shanghai Taipei Toronto

With offices in

Argentina Austria Brazil Chile Czech Republic France Greece Guatemala Hungary Italy Japan Poland Portugal Singapore South Korea Switzerland Thailand Turkey Ukraine Vietnam

OXFORD and OXFORD ENGLISH are registered trade marks of Oxford University Press in the UK and in certain other countries

This edition © Oxford University Press 2011

The moral rights of the author have been asserted

Database right Oxford University Press (maker)

First published in Classic Tales 1995
2015 2014
10 9 8 7 6 5

ISBN: 978 0 19 423930 1

This *Classic Tale* title is available as an e-Book with Audio Pack
ISBN: 978 0 19 423933 2

Also available: Little Red Riding Hood Activity Book and Play
ISBN: 978 0 19 423931 8

Printed in China

This book is printed on paper from certified and well-managed sources.

ACKNOWLEDGEMENTS

Illustrated by: Michelle Lamoreaux/Shannon Associates